The Testing of Hanna Senesh

Hanna Senesh at the kibbutz Sdot Yam, near Caesarea

The Testing of Hanna Senesh

Ruth Whitman

WITH A HISTORICAL BACKGROUND BY
LIVIA ROTHKIRCHEN

WAYNE STATE UNIVERSITY PRESS DETROIT 1986

Library of Congress Cataloging-in-Publication Data

Whitman, Ruth, 1922–
    The testing of Hanna Senesh.

    1. Senesh, Hannah, 1921–1944, in fiction, drama,
poetry, etc.   2. World War, 1939–1945—Poetry.
3. Holocaust, Jewish (1939–1945)—Poetry.   I.
Rothkirchen, Livia.   II. Title.
PS3573.H5T47   1986   811'.54   86-23392
ISBN 0-8143-1853-3
ISBN 0-8143-1854-1 (pbk.)

Grateful acknowledgment is made to the *Croton Review,
Genesis 2, Jewish Frontier,* and *Shirim,* where some of the
poems in this volume originally appeared. "The death
ships" has been reprinted in *Blood to Remember: American
Poets on the Holocaust* by Avon Books.

For my father, Meyer David Bashein

Yet even in death you will have your fame,
to have gone like a god to your fate,
in both your living and dying.

—Sophocles, *Antigone,* ll. 834–836

And let us remember the parachutists, emissaries from Israel,
who were the first to come to the aid of the nations besieged in
Europe, and who did not return.

—Abba Kovner, *Scrolls of Fire*

Contents

Preface

I want to express my thanks for the personal testimony and assistance of Reuven Dafni, who allowed me to interview him for many pleasant hours, and the late Joel Palgi, both of whom were in the parachute rescue mission with Hanna Senesh in 1944; to Hanna's mother and brother, Catherine and Giora (George) Senesh of Haifa, who filled in many details of Hanna's life; and to Miriam Neeman, curator of the Hanna Senesh Archives at Kibbutz Sdot Yam.

I am also grateful to Mishkenot Sha'ananim, the center for artists and writers in Jerusalem, where I began this book in 1977; to the Martin Tananbaum Foundation for two grants that allowed me to visit Israel in 1979 and 1981 to continue my research; and to the Rhode Island State Council on the Arts and the MacDowell Colony of Peterborough, New Hampshire, for supporting me while I did the writing.

Hanna Senesh's most famous Hebrew poem, "Blessed Is the Match," appears in my translation on p. 77. The farewell letter she actually wrote to her mother before her execution, in my translation from the Hebrew, appears on p. 111. (This may not have been her last letter to her mother, since the Hungarian officer who ordered her execution refused to surrender that letter, as well as one written to her comrades in her last hour of life.) All the other poems, as well as the prose passages, are my re-creation of what she might have written during the last nine months of her life.

The Historical Background

LIVIA ROTHKIRCHEN

*H*anna Senesh's life—from 1921 to 1944—spans the most crucial period in recent history, a period that includes the rise of Nazism in Europe and the Second World War. She was twenty-three years old when a firing squad executed her in her native city, Budapest, on November 7, 1944. In sensitive prose and poetry Ruth Whitman explores the last nine months of Hanna's dramatic mission as a British emissary behind enemy lines in Nazi Europe. *The Testing of Hanna Senesh* is a moving imaginative postscript to the diary of the legendary young poet, pioneer, and hero of World War II.

Hanna Senesh was born on July 17, 1921, in Budapest. Her father died when she was still a child, and her mother, Catherine, née Salzberger, became the central figure in Hanna's life. Surrounded by a closely knit family, Hanna was brought up in an elegant and assimilated Jewish milieu which fully identified itself with Hungarian society and was rooted in its cultural heritage. This essay will attempt to trace Hanna's spiritual growth and transformation against the background of the major historical events both in her chosen land of Israel and in her native country, Hungary.

The record of Jewish life in this enclave of East Central Europe reaches back to Hungary's early history. For centuries the Jews of Hungary prided themselves on the knowledge that as far back as the Magyars' national territorial conquest in the tenth century, Jews had resided in this area. Grave inscriptions from Pannonia and Dacia in the Roman period, as well as epitaphs and relics of Jewish settlement in the Middle Ages and during the Turkish occupation of Hungary also provided evidence of Jewish presence in this region.

During the seventeenth century the first Jewish families immigrated to Hungary from neighboring Austria, Bohemia, Moravia, Si-

13

lesia, and Germany. Later, there was a massive influx of immigrants from Galicia and Poland. By the beginning of the eighteenth century, when most of Hungary came under Hapsburg rule, only a few remnants of the ancient Jewish settlements remained. A century later, with the onset of the liberal era, the Jewish population of Hungary experienced a spectacular transformation. As a result of the Emancipation Law of 1867 and a policy of equality and tolerance, Jews came to be respected citizens, sharing fully in the economic and cultural development of the country.

After the First World War and the dissolution of the Austro-Hungarian monarchy, however, the public attitude toward the Jews underwent a radical change. The Treaty of Trianon on June 4, 1920, defined new frontiers: two-thirds of Hungary's territory, with about three million Hungarian nationals, was annexed to Czechoslovakia, Yugoslavia, and Rumania, an event regarded as a national humiliation. By the early twenties there was a strong right-wing anti-Semitic force in the country. The numerus clausus law was enacted by parliament, which set limits on the number of Jewish students allowed to attend institutions of higher learning. Fifty years after the emancipation of the Jews, Hungary became the pioneer in anti-Jewish legislation in Europe.

Nevertheless, many Jewish writers and musicians continued to enjoy popularity within Hungary. In Budapest, ridiculed as "Judapest," Jews comprised 30 percent of the population. The works of talented Jews were translated into several languages and were performed in leading theaters abroad. One of the most popular playwrights was Bela Senesh, known under the pen name of "Coal Man," father of Hanna Senesh.

It was from her father that Hanna inherited her literary talent. With Grandmother Fini's help, Hanna produced her first literary efforts. Six years old, uncertain about the rules of spelling, she dictated her first poems to her grandmother. Later, she and her brother, George, a year older, issued "The Little Senesh Papers," dealing with current affairs and including a special feature on humor. Occasionally, well-known writers, friends of her father, contributed to this journal, among them Zsolt Harsányi.

Life was filled with amusements: excursions to Lake Balaton and the Tatra Mountains, holidays in Italy and France, and concerts, performances, and parties. Hanna's teacher observed at the end of the school year in 1929 that "her imagination is colorful, rich, abounding in ideas. She never fails to fulfil her duty, anxious to accomplish the tasks entrusted to her." A recommendation for entrance to secondary school, issued two years later commented, "Her style and her poems are reminiscent of her father's gift for expression." Her teachers at the exclusive Protestant school recognized her talents by awarding her various literary prizes. In what was considered a special favor, Hanna's mother paid only double tuition for her daughter and not the triple tuition that most Jews had to pay.

Hanna's teens were marked by a growing desire for artistic expression. At the age of thirteen she started a diary, which she kept for ten years. She wrote about her experiences at school and in her family circle and also commented on political events in Hungary and the world. In 1936 she made her first attempt at playwriting with a historical one-act parody, "Bella gerunt alii, tu, felix Austria, nube," a school performance in which she was both actor and director. She wrote four humorous sketches in which suitors from four different historical ages proposed marriage to their loved ones: a B.C.E. suitor; a medieval knight; a petit bourgeois in 1836; and an astronaut in the year 2036 who proposes to a woman astronaut after a flight to Mars. She mentions food tablets and television, apparently influenced by the writings of Huxley. She also wrote thoughtful papers on history and literature, exploring for the first time a Jewish theme in an essay entitled "Jewish References in Hungarian Literature," a prelude to her more mature writings on "Our Nation" and "Zionist Foundations."

The incorporation of Austria into the Reich on March 13, 1938, brought the boundaries of Germany to the gates of Hungary, creating a highly tense political climate in the whole region. Wanting Hitler's favor, the Hungarian government acted quickly to show its sympathy for the "New Order" in Europe by further restricting the rights of the Jews. In April 1938 the "First Jewish Law" was introduced. It was intended to "ensure with greater effectiveness the balance in social and economic life."

The deteriorating status of Jews throughout Europe and the increase in anti-Semitism in her immediate environment stimulated Hanna's interest in Palestine. In the same high school where she had been praised and rewarded, she was now not allowed to keep her elected position as president of the literary society. In late 1938, as Hanna stood on the threshold of her matriculation, she began to find her way toward Jewish consciousness and Zionism. Everything she wrote from this time onwards was colored by her passion for Eretz Israel. On October 26, 1938, she wrote in her diary: "I am a Zionist. That word conveys a lot. I am more aware now of my Jewishness and sense it with all my heart. I am proud of being Jewish and I hope to go to Eretz Israel to help in building up the country. Of course this idea did not come to me overnight. When three years ago I first heard of Zionism I was definitely opposed to it. Now I have land under my feet and a purpose for which it is worthwhile working." Hanna started to learn Hebrew and made up her mind to immigrate to Palestine when she graduated from high school. Before leaving Budapest, she collected photographs and information on the lineage of her family. She compiled this into a booklet, which she intended as a farewell to her past.

The "Second Jewish Law" was put into effect on May 8, 1939. Its main innovations were the reduction of the proportion of Jews in economic and cultural occupations to 6 percent and forbidding Jews to occupy any controlling managerial or influential positions in newspaper offices, theaters, cinemas, film studios, or in the armed forces. A special instruction provided that in war "Jews were to be engaged only in the line of fire." The term "Jew" was redefined as a person whose "parents belonged to the Mosaic faith to the extent of 50 percent," that is, if one or two grandparents were Jews. At this stage, exemptions from the law were still granted to Jewish war veterans who had medals, to invalids, and to Olympic champions.

This new definition of "Jew" on racial grounds resulted in a wave of conversions to Christianity in all the Jewish communities. It is estimated that at the turn of 1938, approximately fourteen thousand Jews converted, in the hope of becoming exempt from the anti-Semitic laws. Many of the outstanding writers, artists, and leading figures of the Hungarian economy became Christian, but in late 1939 it became clear that conversion was no protection against racial persecution.

The outbreak of war on September 1, 1939, the strengthening of the extreme right-wing parties, especially of the Arrow-Cross Party, and the increase of the Jewish population from Hungary's newly acquired areas placed a heavy burden on Jewish community leadership. The leaders of the community in Budapest, reacting to the anti-Jewish laws, issued this declaration: "Hundreds of thousands of Hungarian citizens of Mosaic faith who had always labored for their fatherland and were ready to sacrifice their lives for it, are now being excluded from the national partnership which has been maintained for generations."

In this atmosphere of disappointment and frustration, Hanna decided to leave Hungary. She set out for Palestine on September 19, 1939, on board the *Bessarabia*. Her mother remained behind in Budapest; her brother had already gone to France to study engineering. As soon as she arrived in Haifa, Hanna began study at the Nahalal Agricultural School, eager to learn how to work on the land. In 1940, while she was still a student, she wrote her first poem in Hebrew, on Yom Kippur Eve. At the same time she started to write her diary entries in Hebrew, determined to make it her own language. She consoled herself for her errors: "It is better to write a little in Hebrew than a lot in Hungarian."

In 1941 Hanna joined the young pioneering kibbutz, Sdot Yam, near the ruins of ancient Caesarea. As a member of the settlement she performed various duties: working in the kitchen, the garden, and the laundry, scrubbing floors, tending chickens, and performing guard duty. In her free time she swam in the sea, climbed the rocks, and meditated about the past and future. In Sdot Yam she wrote her most moving poetry.

Much of Hanna's diary is valuable as a chronicle of Palestine during the war. She reported the fate of the refugee ships, news from the European war zone, and the activities of the Yishuv. There is no problem or idea that did not attract her analytic mind. She discussed the future of the kibbutz, the role of the working class in a socialist society. Her one-act play, "The Violin," reflects her own conflict between her artistic aspirations and her commitment to the kibbutz. The heroine, Judith, a talented violinist, faces the choice between collective society and art and decides to devote herself to the collective, since service to the community is a higher and more significant goal than the success of an individual. Obviously, Hanna's commitment was nurtured both by the precarious situation of the Jews in Europe and the thriving, hopeful atmosphere she encountered in Palestine.

During the thirties Jewish colonization in British Mandatory Palestine had made great progress. In the famous words of Minister Malcolm MacDonald: "They have made the desert bloom. They have started a score of thriving industries. . . . They have founded a great city (Tel Aviv) on the barren shore. They have harnessed the Jordan and spread its electricity throughout the land." Ironically, the same MacDonald signed the infamous Statement of Policy known as the White Paper of May 17, 1939, in which the British government limited the number of Jewish immigrants to seventy-five thousand for five years, making the Yishuv dependent in subsequent years on Arab acquiescence. This curtailing of Jewish immigration—a breach of British pledges—was meant to appease the Arabs, but dealt a serious blow to the Yishuv because it sealed off Palestine as a refuge at the moment when the survival of European Jewry was threatened.

With mounting persecution in Germany, the late thirties saw an increase in the stream of refugees, which began with Hitler's advent to power in 1933. The refugees were chiefly Central European Jews—German, Austrian, Czechoslovak, and some Rumanian and Hungarian. They set out from eastern Mediterranean ports on discarded Greek or Turkish cattle boats, leaking tankers, or old freighters, paying exorbitant sums to private entrepreneurs or boat owners for their passage. Some of these "little death ships," as Arthur Koestler described them, sailed clandestinely to Palestine, landing their human cargo by night; others were intercepted by the British navy. In accordance with the White Paper, those caught were brought to Haifa and to the island of Mauritius, or sent back to their ports of embarkation in Europe. The odysseys of the sunken ships *Patria, Pacific, Milos, Struma,* among others, were reported by the survivors of these vessels. Despite British interception, however, the influx of illegal Jewish immigrants grew considerably in the summer of 1939, fostered occassionally by the Irgun Zvi Leumi (the National Military Organization). The British admitted fifty thousand refugees into Great Britain, but feared that a massive exodus to Palestine would provoke the Arabs and thus unbalance the Mandate's policy.

The fall of Mussolini and the turning of the tide on the fronts had, of course, positive repercussions in Mandatory Palestine. Since the fall of 1939, the leadership of the Hagana in Palestine had proposed various plans to the British authorities for the active engagement of a Jewish force. One of the proposals was to provide a Jewish unit of volunteers to operate behind enemy lines in Nazi-occupied Europe. But it was only in late 1943 that the reluctance of the British was overcome and a handful of Palestinian Jews were allowed to participate in this enterprise. The proviso was that "they be used as individuals under SOE [Special Operation Executive]." Most of the young men and women were in their early twenties, each selected for outstanding physical and intellectual qualifications, from the elite stock of the pioneer settlements. The women were recruited into the Women's Auxiliary Air Force and the men into the Buffs or Pioneer Corps.

As the news of the plight of European Jews under Nazi occupation began to leak out to Palestine, Hanna became increasingly worried about the fate of her mother and the Jewish people. Hanna learned about the political developments in Hungary and the fate of the Jews there not only through the media but also through her exchange of letters with her mother. Still living in Buda in the family's villa on Bimbo Street, Hanna's mother described the changes which were affecting the everyday life of the Jews. Then Hanna made a decision. On January 8, 1943, she wrote in her diary: "This week has been most agitating. Suddenly the idea occurred to me: I must go to Hungary, be there at this time, help in organizing Youth Aliyah and bring my mother out." She had heard that the British were organizing volunteers to act behind the enemy lines in Nazi-occupied Europe and was eager to join them: "This is just what I dreamt of . . . I feel herein the hand of destiny, just as before when I left for Palestine. Then, too, I was not the master of my own will. I was caught by an idea that gave me no peace. I knew I would go to Palestine, no matter what obstacles were in my way. This time again I feel the same drive towards an important and necessary task and its inevitability."

She enlisted in the Hagana and prepared herself for her departure for Cairo, where she would receive training with British Intelligence. Before leaving, Hanna copied her Hebrew poems in a notebook, signed them "Hagar"—the code name she was given for her mission—and entrusted the book to Miriam Yitzhaki, her closest friend in the kibbutz.

At that time the Allied forces were in great need of volunteers in the Balkans to help with the rescue of military personnel stranded or imprisoned in enemy-occupied territories. The mission of the Palestinian volunteers was twofold: first, they were to relay to British Intelligence firsthand information regarding enemy strength, location of factories and bridges, and troop movements; second, to organize Jewish resistance, establish rescue centers, and devise means for the evacuation of Jews into liberated partisan territories.

Despite the obvious risks the Jewish emissaries were likely to face in Nazi Europe, the volunteers of the Yishuv were eager to embark on their mission. The situation in early 1944 still seemed favorable for such enterprises. There existed in southeastern Europe a sizeable Jewish population—about one and a half million Jews—the largest diaspora in Hungary and the remnants of Jewry in Slovakia, Rumania, and Bulgaria. Swift actions by guerrilla fighters might have been of great value in these areas. But because of delays and technical obstacles, many precious months had been lost.

Tragically, Hanna and her fellow emissaries arrived in Europe too late. The general turmoil prevailing in southeastern Europe, the drastic security measures employed by the Nazis, and their ferocity in dealing with captured Allied personnel thwarted rescue activities from the outset. The first group of volunteers had landed in Rumania in the fall of 1943. In March 1944, Hanna flew with the other paratroopers, Sergeant Nussbacher (later known as Joel Palgi) and Peretz Goldstein, together with Reuven Dafni, to Bari, Italy; they were assigned to "Operation Chicken I" in Hungary, as it is named in British Intelligence records.

Two days later they parachuted into Slovenia. They stayed in Yugoslavia for about three months with Tito's partisans, waiting to cross into Hungary. They witnessed battles waged by Yugoslav partisans, the destruction of towns and villages by enemy troops, and the plight of the local population. In Srdice Hanna wrote her poem, "Blessed Is the Match," an apotheosis of self-sacrifice, which she gave to Reuven Dafni, who stayed behind in Yugoslavia when she crossed the border.

Meanwhile, in Hungary, events had reached a climax. By March 1944 the German High Command had its plans ready for "Operation Margarethe," the code name for the military occupation of Hungary. On March 12, Eichmann brought his *Sondereinsatzkommando* (Special Task Force, which would eliminate Hungary's Jews) to Mauthausen, Austria, in order to prepare its activities. On March 17 Hungary's regent, Nicolas Horthy, was secretly summoned and persuaded to give his consent to the occupation.

The Anglo-American invasion of Normandy on June 6, 1944, and the advance of the Red Army toward the Carpathian Mountains and the borders of Hungary spurred Eichmann to work feverishly to achieve his final goal—the total removal of all Jews from Hungary. After clearing out the provincial areas, his principal target remained: the capital city, Budapest, with its 220,000 Jews. Their deportation was planned for July. Between June 17 and June 24, more than 20,000 Jews of the city were crammed into buildings marked by the Star of David.

On June 9, 1944, at the height of the deportation of the Jews from the provinces, Hanna Senesh managed to cross the border from Slovenia into Hungary. The next day she was denounced to the Hungarian police by an informer and taken to a Gestapo prison in Budapest. The other two parachutists—Nussbacher and Goldstein—were arrested a short time after their slightly later arrival in Hungary. British Intelligence sources reveal that at one point the comrades were placed in adjacent prison cells. Hanna was able to tap out to Nussbacher a good deal of information before she was taken away for further interrogation and torture.

Meanwhile, two young Jewish escapees from Auschwitz revealed authentic data and figures about the extermination of millions of Jews in the death camps. Members of the Jewish Council brought these so-called "Auschwitz Protocols" to the attention of Regent Horthy. The information eventually reached Switzerland, where it was given wide publicity in July 1944. Both the Catholic and Protestant churches continued to demand an easing of the plight of the persecuted, though their main concern was for the fate of their converts. The reading of a joint pastoral letter that they prepared in protest was delayed for two months, but was finally read as a formal declaration from the pulpits on July 16. By that time, however, five hundred thousand Jews of the provincial areas had already been deported.

At noon on October 15, the very day the Germans kidnapped his son by a ruse, Regent Horthy, in an effort to get Hungary out of the war, announced over Budapest radio that Hungary was proclaiming its armistice with the Allies. Representatives of Hungary and Russia had already signed an agreement in Moscow on October 11. In his address Horthy referred to the Jewish question, "the solution of which the Gestapo had dealt with in its well-known way, against the principles of humanity." But Horthy's attempt to save Hungary failed.

Budapest's Jews were doomed to further suffering. By late in the day on October 15, Szálasi, the nation's new leader, announced on the radio his takeover of power, promising to continue the war on the side of the Reich. On October 17 Eichmann appeared in Budapest to begin the final removal of the Jews. Since rolling stock was not available, the remaining Jews had to travel by foot to the German border. In the rain and cold on November 8, the day after Hanna was executed, the first group of Budapest Jews started on this death march, among them Catherine Senesh, Hanna's mother. It is estimated that about sixty thousand Jews were removed from the capital in this way.

Budapest was filled with confusion and terror. Jews who did not possess protective passports were locked up in a ghetto in Buda. The streets were controlled by the mob, everyone competing for the booty of Jewish property. At every hour of the day Jews could be seen being dragged by men of the Arrow-Cross Party to some unknown destination, usually a dark cellar or the banks of the Danube, where thousands of people were shot. The Russians had begun their systematic bombing of Budapest; the city was under siege and the terror increased. At the end of December Otto Komoly, president of the Zionist Federation, was kidnapped by the Arrow-Cross and vanished. Jews in hiding places were constantly in danger; children were hidden in orphanages and monasteries. The Swedish rescue team headed by Raoul Wallenberg, and including Professor Waldemar Langlet and his wife, Nina, Asta Nilson, and other righteous Gentiles, among them individual priests and nuns, risked their lives to save the remnant of Budapest's Jewry. One part of the city, Pest, fell to the Soviet army on January 18, 1945.

Buda became free on February 13. The gardens in the ghetto, the courtyards of the Jewish Council offices, and the ritual baths were covered with heaps of cadavers, victims of the Nazis' last vengeance.

The liberation of Budapest came too late for many and too late for Hanna Senesh. On October 28, after four months in the Budapest prison, whe was tried by a Hungarian military court. American bombers were pounding the city, and Soviet guns could be heard on the outskirts of Budapest. Although she had not received an official sentence, Hanna was executed by a firing squad on November 7. Her execution was ordered by a Hungarian officer, Captain Simon, who acted on his own initiative. Peretz Goldstein, her fellow parachutist, perished in one of the concentration camps. Only Nussbacker, Joel Palgi, survived, managing to escape from a locked deportation train. He made his way back to Budapest, dug up the transmitter he had buried when he arrived, and was able to communicate for a few weeks with headquarters in Britain.

Hanna's last days were recalled by some of her fellow prisoners and parachutists who survived and by the Hungarian guards who came into contact with her during her imprisonment. Her mother, who was jailed for a time in the same prison and, through the goodwill of some of the guards, was occasionally permitted to meet with Hanna, has written her reminiscences of that harrowing period. Eyewitnesses related that during one point in Hanna's trial, everyone was asked to leave the courtroom, and Hanna was left alone with the judges. It was reported that she presented her own defense boldly, analyzing the moral decline of Hungary in siding with Nazi Germany and warning that those participating in the crime would pay for it. She refused to ask for clemency from "hangmen and murderers."

Since the Jewish Burial Society was no longer functioning in Budapest, Hanna's body was buried by merciful Gentiles in the martyr's section of the Jewish cemetery. After the establishment of the State of Israel, Hanna Senesh's remains were transferred to Jerusalem and buried on Mount Herzl in the Military Cemetery beside fellow parachutists who were also executed in Europe. A mourning nation paid its tribute to the young woman who would become a legend. Since then, monuments have been erected in her memory throughout the country. Farming settlements, a ship, a forest, several streets, and a species of flower now bear her name.

On November 2, five days before Hanna was executed, Bill Tone, a British officer serving with the partisans in Yugoslavia, wrote to a friend in Jerusalem: "I had the pleasure of meeting a young woman from

Palestine, who parachuted to my headquarters in Slovenia and proceeded overland to another part of Europe. She was a grand girl and as plucky as anyone could be. Should you hear of her when she returns, please put yourself out to meet her. She was accompanied by two other men from Palestine. They were all excellent and will be regarded as great heroes as time goes on."

Hanna's literary legacy became public domain after the war. Her diary and poems have been translated into many languages, and some of her poems have been set to music; several have been recorded and are often played. They are now part of the folk heritage of Israel. On January 11, 1944, before embarking on her mission, Hanna Senesh wrote the last entry in her diary: "I want to believe that what I have done, and will do, are right. Time will tell the rest." She could never have imagined that forty years later an American poet would pick up the thread of her life and would spend several years in the effort to relive and recreate her last days with so much empathy and insight.

As a little child
I heard a voice

calling me, commanding me:
it was dim at first,

but I knew I was chosen:
it called me, called

until I followed:
now I hear it clearly:

I must be the match
to strike the flame:

I must be the flame

I
BUDAPEST

JUNE 1944

They've been beating me for three days.

My ribs ache.
I think my wrist is broken.
And my jaw is throbbing where the police
knocked out a tooth.

The Gestapo agent was furious
when I threw the book of French poems out of the train
and tried to jump after.
He didn't know the transmitter code was in the book,
he was just angry that I tried to escape.

Now I can't tell anyone the code, even if I wanted to.

After the first shock
it's like letting a wave of flame singe your hand:
first a sharp sensation, then no feeling.
I watch myself like a person in a dream
while they invent devices to break me down.

But I never scream.
Screaming means it's happening to me.
I step back and watch it happen around me.

Anger helps. Anger makes a barrier between the whip and me.
They tie me up
and beat my soles, my palms, my back:
                                        I say

no no to myself
don't let them have a sign that I feel it:

think of the blue-green sea that I saw every night
from my tent under the old stars,
the cool winds of evening:

think of that hill in Jerusalem,
the little lights shining in the villages,
breathe the aromatic Judaean air,
watch the sun set over the Old City,
the shadows creeping up the towers,
pulling the bruised light behind them:

you see: I feel nothing.

It is only my body flopping like a fish.

It is only my body that bleeds.

the self
becomes small and thin
a single taper
burning
          in immense darkness

In this small cell on the top floor of the prison
I count:
       chair,
             bed,
                    table.
The window is high and horizontal, out of reach.
I push the bed beneath it,
lift the table with my aching arms,
and place the chair on top.

I climb up and stand on the peak of my shaky mountain.
Now I can see sky, trees,
even the street where I once lived—
Bimbo Street.
But that was long ago and another me.

Four Gestapo policemen are taking me to Military Headquarters
on Horthy Miklos Boulevard.
They won't tell me why.
I'm sitting with my eyes closed,
trying not to feel the throbbing of my bruises,
the pain in my head.

I imagine I hear my mother's voice.
The door of the room opens,
a large man steps out and says.
"Bring the girl in."

The police push me roughly through the door.
My mother is standing there.
I break out of their hands and fly into her arms.
For the first time, I let my tears come.

"Mother! Forgive me!"

My mother, my beautiful mother has aged, her hair is gray.

"Aniko, what has happened to you?

What have they done to your poor face?
Why?"

"Yes," says Mr. Rozsa, the civilian interrogator,
"tell your mother why you're here.
We'll leave you two alone."

"Aniko, did you come back because of me?
I could never forgive myself for that."

"No, I hoped you were already in Palestine with George."

"Then why, why?
Didn't you know the Germans were in Hungary?
Look at your bruises, your skin, your hurt wrists.
They've even knocked out a tooth!"

She begins to embrace me, weeping, and the men rush in.

"No secrets!" they shout.

Rosza says, "Now tell us what you were doing
with the transmitter, or watch us
torture your mother."

I look at my mother and see
although she doesn't understand what I'm doing here,
she trusts me. She doesn't flinch.

"I have nothing to say."

They take me away.

Trapped in this gray square
I know the earth
is moving across the dawn
from meridian to meridian

all night I keep watching,
searching the walls, the floor
for an opening
into the light:

dreams stream down my face,
my breath stops in my throat,
my bones crush against each other

as I beat at my own absence

A round reflection of sunlight flickers on my ceiling.
At first I think it's accidental, but it moves around.
Then I realize it is being done on purpose,
with a mirror.

Someone is talking to me.

This afternoon, when the sun is on my side,
I'll try to answer.

Behind my closed lids I see
the late afternoon sun
shining through the petals
of a red flower:
a transparent red light
as though the petals
were of glass
except for the shadow
that falls across them
and the secret black center

II
YUGOSLAVIA

MARCH 1944 TO JUNE 1944
THREE MONTHS EARLIER

Sitting in the dark inside the plane,
I hear the dispatcher dumping the bales,
each attached to its own parachute.

It's bright moonlight.
we're over Slovenia, which has just been liberated
from the Germans.
                        The partisans
are expecting us. Below I can see
the fires marking the letter E
to show us their position.

It's time to jump.

Every fiber in my body is against it.
But I know that when I let go,
when I let myself fall into open space,
I burst open my limits and feel I can do anything.

The hatch opens.

I jump against the moon.

―2―

Stepping out,
I'm delivered to air:
I'm swept into turbulence,
tumbling down
past twenty-five feet
of nowhere:

the laws and patterns of space
unfold my arms and legs:

my parachute blossoms,
a spray of the milkweed,
as my pendulum body
swings beneath it:

now I'm falling slowly,
alive:
I see the trees below me:
I come to the end of sky,
stem first,
ballooning   then collapsing
flower   string   wind:

I cut the cord
and the world is mine

I land on six feet of snow in the moonlight.
It's like falling into a featherbed.

The wind has blown me off course
and I've floated away from the others, out of sight.
As I jumped behind Reuven I heard him curse the pilot
for dropping us on the wrong side of the wind,
away from the flaming E.

I blow the whistle they gave me.
The sound cuts across the silence.
Tall Yugoslav mountains are all around me,
nothing but snow and rock.

Reuven and Abba come out of a patch of trees, shouting,
"There she is!"
We hug each other, laughing with relief.

A band of strange men appear and come towards us,
holding rifles.
Reuven puts his hand on his grenade,
in case we've been betrayed to the Nazis.
But then we see the men are wearing red stars on their caps.

They're Tito's partisans.

Standing in the snow, they are barefoot.

4

The Germans have marched into Budapest.

What will become of the million Jews in Hungary?
They'll be killed by the Nazis while we sit here in the snow.

"Reuven," I say, trying not to cry with disappointment,
"What about the plans we made
to help the refugees escape to Palestine?
Let's cross the border now, quickly,
before the Germans bring the storm troopers."

"No," he says, "it's hopeless.
We tried to reach Budapest before the Germans,
but they were too fast for us."

"You mean we were too slow," I say bitterly.
"Why didn't the British arrange to drop us sooner?
The longer we wait, the more impossible it will be.
Let's cross the border now."

"No, Hanna," he says, "it's too late.
You'll only be endangering all of us
and then there'll be no one left
to contact the underground."

"I don't care. It's better to take the risk now
than never to try at all. How can you
sit back and do nothing?"

"That's enough," he says, getting angry.
"You'll get us all wiped out if you keep on like this."

"But we must cross the border. And find a new escape route.
Yugoslavia, Hungary, Rumania, are all being shut off.
How can we reach the ships
that will carry the refugees to Palestine
unless we go now?"

I remember the battered ship
that waited for months in the Turkish harbor
and was never allowed to land:

6

The death ships. The Struma.
*It lay in the harbor at Istanbul
without food or coal.*

*Don't let it land,
said the Ambassador.*

*Jews are enemy aliens,
said the British.
Tow them out to the Black Sea,
send them to Crete, Mauritius,
to Rumania, Germany, Jamaica,
but don't let them come to Palestine.*

That was December 1941.

*Safe in my kibbutz at Sdot Yam
(meadows of the sea),*
                    *I looked
at the peacock-blue Mediterranean
and cried, let them come,
we have room.*

*No, said Lord Moyne,
if one ship comes
they'll all want to come.*

Let the children come.

*Children?
What will we do with children?*

*The hold was airless.
Sickness, filth,
layers of excrement, vomit.*

44

The ship could not sail.
The ship could not stay.
No land would take them.

In February the ship exploded
outside the harbor at Istanbul.
Eight hundred lives flew up,
their rags, arms, legs, hopes,
falling like rain.

One was saved.
He was allowed to enter
Palestine.

We're hiding in the forest near Semič.
The Germans keep pushing us south
through woods and mountains.

I've had my hand on my pistol several times,
but haven't fired it yet.
                              I try not to think of
soft human flesh.
When we trained in Cairo, we shot wooden dummies.
But a man, even an enemy, is real, with blood,
thoughts, hopes.
                         How can I destroy that?

We haven't changed our clothes or had a bath
since we joined the partisans.
                                    I never expected
to live like this, playing hide and seek
with Nazi murderers in the mountains of Yugoslavia.

Reuven and I have hardly spoken since our quarrel.
He knows I'm determined to find a way
to cross the border,
even if I have to do it alone.

Every day we walk farther away from the Slovenian border.
Now we're moving into Croatia.

One part of my mind watches for an enemy patrol.
The other part notices the white birches around us,
the long trunks of pines, the poplars by the streams.

Even now, part of me observes with a cool eye.

I think of the pine tree
beside my tent
on the dune
at kibbutz Sdot Yam:

I watched the sea,
I walked on the fragrant shore
and my blood lifted
with the salty lift of the tide:

now under the pine trees
in a foreign land
I live day and night
with strangers:

I'm a drop of oil on water,
sometimes floating,
sometimes sinking,
but always apart

=10=

Everywhere I go the partisans are startled to see me.
Perhaps it's my British Air Force uniform.

Last night there was a party in a village
of lavender-painted houses.
                              The men and women
came into the meeting house, laid down their rifles,
and began to dance and sing.
Someone had a gusla, a kind of Yugoslavian guitar,
and we clapped to the music as the dancers danced.
I danced most of the night.
The table was heaped with cheese, bread, pancakes,
cherries, peaches, wine, slivovitz,
but I was too excited to eat.

They asked me to say a few words to our comrades.
I stood on a table and shouted,
"Death to Fascism! Freedom to the people!"
holding my fingers in a V.

They clapped and cheered.
I could see that Reuven was pleased with me for once.
He smiled and touched my shoulder.

Surrounded by Nazi patrols hunting for us,
we crouch in the forest for ten hours,
not daring to speak or breathe,
afraid the flutter of a leaf will betray us.

When we huddle in the bushes like this,
when we can't even whisper among ourselves,
I've learned to let my mind wander out of my body
to other times and places.
                    Hiding here in the mud and twigs
I remember how I used to take care of the cows
when I first arrived in Palestine.

Shoveling manure in the barn
I breathe the heavy acrid smell
of cows' excrement:
it is not so unpleasant,
it is full of sharp hay and grass
and fields of sweet clover

But the pile is a mountain,
soft and endlessly yielding:
I reach across with my shovel
and my foot gives way
as I slide into it
up to my waist

At that moment
my whole life changes

The dainty schoolgirl,
the airy pioneer
who used to play Chopin
with delicate white fingers
begins to laugh
and curse the cows
in salty Hungarian

13

Thinking of my arms and legs covered with manure,
I begin to laugh, and Reuven shushes me sternly.

The forest is finally clear,
and we can crawl out of the underbrush.
My legs are so cramped it takes a while to unbend them.
I can hardly walk.

=14=

An uneasy wind
blows through the trees
bending the tall pines;
one small bird
flies over my head,
chirps a warning,
then hides in the leaves

We're resting in a cave with the partisans.
It's a radio station, a hideout with food and medicine.
Marking time again.

Here in Croatia the partisan general
has asked us not to tell the fighters
that we are Palestinian Jews.
Our British uniforms would convince them—
what they've already been told—
that the Jews rule Britain. So when we speak
Hebrew among ourselves,
we tell them we're speaking Welsh and they believe us.

With nothing to do,
I start to think about September 1939,
when I left Hungary for Palestine.
The Germans had invaded Poland. The war had started.
I took the train from Budapest to the mouth of the Danube
in Rumania, where I caught the *Bessarabia,* bound for Haifa.

Haifa. Overhead the crown of Mount Carmel
above the Mediterranean;
the port, gold in the sun, was crowded with ships,
the streets full of excited men and women,
loud voices, extravagant gestures.

I went south from Haifa to Tel Aviv—
a new city built on sand dunes—
and up through orange groves leaning fragrant
in the arms of cypresses
along the narrow road to the Judaean hills,
up and around until I saw
Jerusalem, the Old City and the new,
a halo of diamonds above the desert.

Then across the desert to the Dead Sea
and the fortress of Masada
where the last remnant of free Jews
was trapped by the Romans
two thousand years ago.

In the end,
when the Romans were climbing up the walls,
the men killed their wives and their children:
then they killed themselves.

I sit here in the mountains of Yugoslavia,
breathing the hot dry air of Masada.

In the midst of the Judaean desert
Masada rises, rock fortress
streaked with tan, brown,
the colors of thirst.

A hot wind blows.

Crows cut across the air below me,
their corrugated cries
the only sound
in the ancient stillness.

King Herod's bath, once a mikva
for the Jews who hid here,
bakes in the heat.
Tails of field mice

flick between a jumble of rocks:
the paint in the throne room dims,
victors and victims
shrivel to dust

=19=

The Germans are moving Jews from the towns outside Budapest
into ghettos, to round them up and deport them.

An eighty-four-year-old woman was dragged from the operating
table where her foot was being amputated. She was thrown
bleeding into a wagon. Her son tried to shoot himself, blew off half
his face, and was hurled in the wagon with his mother.

Where is my mother, my brave mother,
who let me leave her behind in Budapest?
It is the end of April,
we've been wandering for more than a month,
and I'm farther from her than ever.

=20=

We're taking our first bath, here in Čazma,
in a house with running water.

Reuven has found two Allied pilots who were shot down.
He draws maps for them, showing them how
to get to the Adriatic coast
where British boats will come over from Brindisi
and take them to southern Italy.

"Reuven," I say, "don't spend your time
looking for British or American flyers.
Let's cross the border now. Let's save
the Jews who are being hunted in Hungary."

"Hanna, Hanna," he says sadly, "you must be patient.
We can't take foolish risks. We must wait
until we have some chance of success.
And we must keep our promise to the British
to help Allied pilots get back safely."

He makes me angry.
                    Doesn't he realize
we're the ones who must make way,
who must keep the escape routes open?

Root cells.
At the farm at Nahalal
I learned how those pioneer cells
go first into the earth:

they make a way
for the root that follows
so the plant may bloom:
and then the root cells die.

22

Joel, my special friend,
has been dropped into Yugoslavia to join us.

We played together in Cairo while we trained with the British. Joel
taught me how to shoot a pistol. We learned how to take apart and
repair the transmitter, to translate the code, to repel an attacker. After
class we'd go sightseeing: to the pyramids, the zoo, the theater. We
wandered around the city, holding hands.

I love his pixie smile, his arched brows, his intense blue eyes. He looks
like a hero.

I know he has a sweetheart somewhere—perhaps many
sweethearts.

But now there's not time for that.
I feel a different love. I'm burning with it,
this terrible need to give myself to this mission,
to justify my being here.

23

I remember the two Polish women
who came to Palestine
escaped from a death camp
and the news they brought:

some did not believe,
but I knew:

now I follow a path
back to the fiery center

to rescue a live ember

We watch a fight between an American plane
and a German Messerschmidt.
                              Both are shot down.
The American plane falls near us.
We rush over and find the pilot unconscious
but alive.
              Some German tanks
have seen him fall and start coming towards us.

We run through the underbrush, carrying the wounded pilot,
and come to a large underground hospital. The pilot
sips some brandy and says some words in English to Reuven.

In a corner I see the partisans are gathered
around a young girl with a shattered leg. The woman doctor
works with a saw because she has no instruments.
And no anesthetic, only brandy.

I can't bear to look. The girl makes no sound.
I think, if she is brave enough to bear it,
I must be brave enough to comfort her.
I take her hand and watch the tears
run silently down her cheeks.

25

We're sick with diarrhea, we're covered with lice.
The British promise to send us new uniforms
from Brindisi by parachute.

The orchards are now blossoming and the May woods
are alive with young oak trees and mauve crocuses.
The sun is so warm we take off our heavy uniforms
and spread them out to catch the fleas and lice.
Heat makes the insects sleepy.

I stretch out on the ground behind some bushes.
My skin feels the sun.

I know I'm not pretty, my face is too round,
but I have large blue-green eyes and thick curly hair.
And Joel says my long legs are well-shaped.

Will I ever feel a lover's hand on me?
I know, I feel sure there is someone
somewhere in the world as clever as my father,
as cheerful as my brother, as generous as my mother,
waiting for me.

Will I live long enough?

I remember swimming at Lake Balaton
when I was fourteen:

the sand felt warm and smooth
as I waded in:
I lay on my back
and floated on top of the world.
I closed my eyes,
felt the sun on my face.

I picked a cluster
of dark blue ripening grapes
from a vine on the hillside:
bit into a plump warm grape
and the sharp juice
gushed into my mouth:

and I thought of the lake,
how it held me up,
touching me gently everywhere,
how the sun kissed my face.

We've now managed to keep out of reach of the Germans
for almost two months, but Reuven says we still
can't cross the border.

The partisans share their food and shelter with us
but won't give us papers from their huge document factory
and won't let us deal with their chief operators.
They still don't trust us.

I worry, "What will become of our people in Hungary?
We have no right to sit here doing nothing.
No right not to go."

Joel says, "There's no logic in going now."

"This is no time for logic. I'd rather try and fail
than go back home, safe and selfish. Even if we fail,
word will get to them that they're not abandoned,
their suffering is known. That someone at least
risked her life to help them."

"Yes," said Joel, "but if you are captured
it will be a terrible waste. Don't be so obsessive.
You're sometimes very stubborn. That makes life hard
for the rest of us. Please, Hanna,
try to be patient."

"I have been patient," I shout, "I've been patient
for two years, since I first asked the Hagana
to let me join the parachutists.
                    I'm tired of waiting.
Now it's time to act."

He is silent.

28

As I was waking up this morning I heard an explosion in my head, as though a light bulb flew apart inside my brain. Behind my eyes white slivers of glass burst through the black air. Was I dying?

I woke, my heart pounding, terrified.

I keep hearing tree branches snapping inside my head. It's hard to breathe. My heart beats like a hammer, even when I lie still.

Perhaps I'm not equal to this task. I feel breakable, as though my heart, my breath, may stop at any moment.

The trees, my hands, the faces of my comrades look unreal. The whole world distant and transparent.

I lie on the ground all day, not wanting to eat, not wanting to talk.

The middle of May.
The partisans say the way is now clear
and we can move north toward Hungary.
I still feel weak and sick, but I know I must go.
I will cross alone. Joel will cross later.

It's a rainy night.
We're sitting together, waiting near the airfield.

The partisans are singing around the fire.
Joel and I whisper together, remembering
Jewish partisans singing songs of Eretz Israel.
I want to share my heart with him.
I ask him to come and walk with me in the darkness.

We're going to part and I want to remember this moment.

I say to him, "I know I'm headstrong and stubborn
and I sometimes make Reuven angry,
but I want you to understand me."

He puts his arm around me and says,
"Hanna, don't worry. I know how soft and sweet
you really are."

His arm is warm on my shoulder.
I kiss him, a kiss that perhaps is sweeter
to me than to him.

We agree to meet in two weeks
at the Great Synagogue in Budapest.

30

I'll cross the border into Hungary
and find my mother
and lead her to safety.

31

*Braided together,
my mother and I
became strong through loss:
she watched my father die
in the bloom of their love,
and her mother, queen of the house,
sicken and slip away.
And then, skillful at parting,
she parted from me.*

*She let me go, knowing
I would carry her in me
even as she once held me safe
inside her own flesh.*

*Why then, with her center
in me, this tie
across time and distance,
across death itself,
do I have a longing
so sharp
it digs a hollow
beneath my heart?*

32

I'm dining with a partisan general
who has invited me to come to his cave.
He wants to see the girl who insists
on crossing the border into Hungary.

He serves me beef roasted on a spit,
arranged on a platter of branches and leaves.
It's the first meat I've seen for weeks.
I stuff myself shamelessly.

He warns me my mission will end in disaster.

33

The partisans are using wagons and oxen
to cart our guns and provisions.
We have to keep moving.
I'm learning to sleep while walking behind the wagon.
I rest my arms on the back of the cart, put down my head,
and my legs move behind automatically.

The roads are muddy from the late spring thaw.
Some roads are flooded.
I trudge along, my legs caked with mud
up to my knees.

34

We meet two young Jews escaped from the Budapest roundup.
They have just managed to come across the border.
They're on their way to Palestine
with a French prisoner of war named Ivan.

We beg the boys to guide me back.
But they hesitate.
                    They're lucky to escape
this far, and they want to go on to Palestine.
We finally persuade them
just to take me across the Hungarian border.

Reuven is worried. He says, "Your documents
are obviously counterfeit. Why not wait
until we persuade the partisans
to give us better documents?"

I say, "I know it's dangerous.
But I have to go."

I can see he is upset and irritated.

"Then go," he sighs, "I know I can't stop you."

35

There's a fire in me:
it must not go to waste.

Sitting in the snow,
I fan it with my breath.

I cup it in my hands:
it must not be lost.

I am the fire.
I am the moth.

We're in Apatovač, on the border
between Yugoslavia and Hungary.
It's seven in the evening, the ninth of June.
The three men and I are setting out
from this frontier village. We'll hide until morning
then make a dash for Nagykaniza
and the eight o'clock train for Budapest.

I hand Reuven a scrap of paper,
a poem I've written, saying, "If I don't come back,
bring this to my comrades at Sdot Yam."

"I'll wait for you," he says.

The four of us—the two boys, the Frenchman
and I—have a map and a compass.
We cross over to a little village.
Ivan and I hide in a cornfield
while the two boys go to look around.

A Hungarian policeman sees them wandering about
and arrests them for vagrancy. He says
he wants to examine their documents.

One of the boys panics and shoots himself.

The police send word to the Gestapo,
who have been watching every move we make.
A peasant points out where we two are hiding.

A detective pulls me off the ground.
He slaps my face and knocks out my tooth.
He wants me to tell him the radio code
I'm carrying in my book of French poems.

But I am iron.

37

Perhaps I'm not iron.

At first I felt nothing could bend me,
but now I'm not so sure.
They laughed at me when I said I was shot down.
They know I've been with the partisans.

They keep beating the palms of my hands,
the soles of my feet.
They keep asking for the transmitter code.

I'm not sure I can stand more beatings.
The detective twists my arm,
telling me I am now state property.
I say I am no one's property.

Blessed is the match that burns and kindles fire,
blessed is the fire that burns in the secret heart.
Blessed are the hearts that know how to stop with honor . . .
blessed is the match that burns and kindles fire.

III
BUDAPEST

1

A Gestapo prison guard named Hilda,
a friendly Hungarian who was born in Germany,
whispers to me when she brings my food
that Joel is here.

So Joel was caught too.
Perhaps it is he who sends me those little circles
of sunlight across the courtyard every morning.
If only I could talk to him!
I ask Hilda to bring me a mirror.

I will signal to him somehow.
I will light up the black center.

=2=

Mother is in the prison.

Hilda tells me to stand on the chair tower
in front of my window and look across the courtyard.
And there is my mother, waving to me sadly.

I want so much to give her something,
some encouragement, some love.

I look at the dust on the window and slowly, with my forefinger,
I draw four Hebrew letters, as big as I can:
shin, lamed, vav, mem—shalom.

She smiles, not understanding.
And then I decide, I will teach her Hebrew.
But how? Something will come to me.

Four letters of the alphabet
sit on my windowsill
like birds in migration:

four sparrows who spiraled
out of the south
on luminous air:

they rest briefly here
before they travel
their half-arc north:

the letters are white
fragments that gather together:
the word is a blessing,

a connecting ribbon
I fling like confetti
across the void

It is to me the Word is speaking

In the evening Hilda comes and whispers
mother is waiting in the bathroom near my cell.
I rush into the room
while Hilda keeps watch in the corridor.

Mother's thin face is full of joy
at seeing me. We hold each other close,
then look at each other. I take her hands and see
her wrist is bandaged.

"What have they done to you?"

"No, no, it's not what you think. It's nothing."
"You're hurt!"
                "No," she says, "I did it myself.
I was full of despair, the night they brought me here.
Some women in the cell woke and found me,
and stopped the blood. It's nothing. I've forgotten
that moment of weakness.
                                    But what about you,
darling girl? What happened to your tooth?
What are they doing to you? Why are you here?"

"I'm a parachutist for the British.
They sent me here on an intelligence mission
to get in touch with the underground for them,
but I wanted to come mostly to help our people
escape to Palestine.
If all I lose is a single tooth, it's worth it."

Hilda knocks on the door
and we must go back to our cells.

5

July seventeenth. My twenty-third birthday.
Sometimes I thought I would never live this long.

What have I accomplished? Nothing.
All my plans, my mission, all have come to nothing.
If only the Russians would enter the city,
we would gather up the survivors,
set the old escape routes in motion,
and start the exodus to Palestine.
But will there be anyone left to save?

Hilda brings birthday gifts from mother:
a jar of marmalade made from Haifa oranges,
a handerkerchief, a sliver of soap, a sponge.

I am rich.

I climb up on my bed-table-chair tower
and draw a Star of David on the window
to thank her.

The sunny taste of these Haifa oranges
remind me of my last night in Haifa
before I left for Cairo.
George had just arrived in port
the night I was supposed to leave.
He looked at my British uniform, puzzled and worried.

"Don't worry," I said, "I'll be back soon
and then I'll tell you everything.
You must go to the kibbutz and wait for mother."

We sat above the bay and watched the lights
of Haifa over the water.

the city
is a crescent of light
curved around the bay

the evening sea and sky
merge into
one dusky surface

only the reflection
of a single small boat—
a night fisherman

alone on the water—
defines the difference
between sky and sea

We walk for ten minutes every day in a circle in the
prison courtyard. Because I'm still in solitary, I'm not
allowed to walk with the other prisoners, but must walk
behind them.

I see that there are children among us and I wave and smile
to them across the circle. Poor things, there is nothing
for them to do all day in this terrible place.

If only I had paper and string, something to write with, I
would make them some toys.

Hilda brings me a few pieces of paper,
a pair of scissors and some colored crayons.
I can't imagine how she got them.

Now I can make paper dolls, little doll pioneers
for the Polish children I see in the courtyard.

Out of thin tissue, hand in hand,
small shapes of boys and girls stand in a row.

I poke my finger through the skin of their world:
it is all made of paper. A puff of breath

could blow it away, could blow away these walls.
Walking up to death, I know I'd find

a hole in the shallow dark, a tear in the veil.
Now my eyes can see the truth of stones:

they are brittle and flat. Transparent. Paper thin.

10

Today in the courtyard, by stopping every few feet
to fix an imaginary shoelace,
                              I lose my place
at the end of the line and manage to come beside mother.

She squeezes my hand and whispers, "How are you?"

"I'm fine, mother."

"Aniko, tell me really why you're here.
What have you done?"

"Mother, I have done nothing wrong.
If the Nazis consider me a criminal,
that's their law, not mine.
When the war is over, what I've done will be
praised and celebrated, I promise you."

I can see she's not convinced.

"Be careful," she says. "You're dearer to me
than my own life."

Marietta, the cruelest of the matrons,
stands in the yard and cracks her whip,
making us run around in a circle,
faster and faster.

Later, I'm in my cell, standing on my tower,
spelling out the Hebrew words to mother,
when Marietta bursts in, shouting
that she has caught me signaling, which proves
I'm a spy, and when she tells the guards,
I'll certainly be shot.

"I'm not a spy," I shout back at her,
"I'm teaching my mother the Hebrew alphabet."

She's astonished, stops for a moment, then stalks out.

12

I never see Joel. They keep
the men and women apart. But we two talk
every day with mirror language.

13

My circle of fire—
a kiss—

          moves on your ceiling,
          its borrowed light

speaking to you
and your circle comes

          yellow as a yolk
          a buttercup moving

across my wall,
speech of the sun

          I try to translate:
          I want to grasp it

with my fingers,
press it against

          my breasts until
          each syllable of light

enters me

          our sun-shadows
          our two worlds

of reflected fire
no longer separate

14

They've put me in a cell with the children.
I dreamed once of teaching children in a classroom,
or having children of my own.
But now I know this will never happen.

I'm teaching the little ones to read and write.
I teach them songs and their eyes shine
as they lift their thin voices. They'd forgotten
they could sing.

The grownups come and want to learn the words.
There is a place, I promise, waiting for them.

15

Today is my mother's twenty-fifth wedding anniversary.
I remember the picture she used to show us
after father died: the two of them
sitting on a bench in our garden
on Bimbo Street, my mother like a young girl,
reading a book, perhaps a book my father
had written—and he beside her, elegantly
dressed in a jacket and white trousers.
Now that world is completely destroyed.

I cover an empty can with silver foil
and insert twenty-five straws from my mattress.
On each straw I paste a paper flower
so it looks like a bouquet of white roses.
I make a little bride to hold
the tissue paper bouquet.

There's no bridegroom. Not for her, not for me.

16

*I am already
the widow of my life:*

*I chose a way separate
but paved with light,*

*a promise that I would be
a gift accepted,*

*that the world and I
would join rejoicing:*

*but now I am
married to solitude,*

*sister of death,
a gift that went astray*

Joel and I are being transferred to a Hungarian prison.
As I come down the stairs I see him waiting in the hall.

"Joel!" I cry and reach out to touch him.
The Gestapo officer roars, "Silence!"
and pulls out his pistol.

We're pushed into the same van, which takes us
to Margit Boulevard Prison.
There the guards are cordial, even fawning.
Joel and I ask if we can talk together,
and they agree to give us half an hour.

I want to hug him, I'm so happy to see him.
He tells me when he reached Budapest,
he was shadowed constantly by the police.
They arrested him and took him to the Hill
for questioning. They tortured him until
he felt he couldn't stand it any more.
He found an aluminum disk left behind
in the cell of an American flyer
and cut his wrists.
                    But the jailers found him,
revived him, and went on with their questioning.

"They know they're in trouble now," Joel says.
"When the Germans surrender the Allies will hold them
responsible for the Jewish massacres.
Now they want to protect themselves,
and that should be to our advantage."

But now our time is up.

"You're still lovely," he says, holding my hands.
"You look thinner, more experienced. It becomes you."

=18=

The Hungarian police have set mother free.

She brings me warm clothes and some cheese and bread.
And my little sewing set I used to play with
when I was a child, sitting on a low stool
beside her chair.
                    We cry and kiss each other,
thinking of those lost times.

I ask her to find me a Bible in Hebrew.
I need those words to remind me
there is a language, a white lightning
to pierce this blackness.

19

They tell me my trial is set for October twenty-eighth.
Mother has found a lawyer who will defend me.
He says he feels sure I'll be released
when the war is over. There's no question
of a death sentence.

~~20~~

My cell is getting colder and colder.
The soup is now nothing but thin gruel.
I'm always hungry.

I lie on my bed and let visions
of the Haifa market rise behind my eyes.

a fist of life
thrusts up through sand
and opens its palm:

a rainbow of vegetables:
black olives, seas of oranges,
eggplants, shiny purple,
artichokes, small
scarlet tomatoes, parsley
curled in bushes
raisins garlic cumin

seeds fall through the air:
the sun is a cauldron
of hot oil

22

Not to despair, not to be diminished.

I'm driving with Joel along the Dead Sea:
shining turquoise on one side of us;
on the other, dusty mountains, muscle and sinew:

we come to the oasis where ibexes run
at Ein Gedi among the palm trees;
we climb up through a green cavern,

up stone steps carved out of the mountain
and come to the first waterfall, the lowest,
pouring out of a cave:
                              thirsty, hot,

we run through the drops, laughing, chasing each other:
we climb through underbrush, along a winding
uphill slope to the second waterfall,

a heavier pouring: we let the cool
fingers comb us:
                    above, the spring begins
at the top of the mountain:
                              we push each other up
to the pool of David, where we swim and loll
as the third waterfall gushes diamonds
over our eyes, our backs:

we stop at noon in the airless shade
of a thorn tree and break open the watermelon
we bought in the Bedouin market:

we break the melon open
and the pink meat fills our mouths with juice,
the sweet liquid gives us back

our strength under the gray beaten thorn tree.

24

They're bringing me into the court. The judge says:

"Hanna Senesh, do you plead guilty to the charge of being a spy,
a traitor to Hungary?"

"I'm guilty only of returning to Hungary to save it from the crime
of destroying its own people."

"Didn't you come in the uniform of a British officer,
wearing the disguise of a secret agent?"

"I am a British officer from Palestine."

"You're lying. You are a Hungarian traitor. You could
save your life, even this late, if you would tell us the code you used
for sending military secrets to the Allies."

"What would you do with the code, even if I had it?
The Germans are running away, the Russians are in the suburbs
of Budapest. You Hungarian Nazis are the real traitors.
Would you use the code to tell the Allies to stop
bombing Budapest? No one would believe you."

"The prisoner is insubordinate, incorrigible, and guilty.
Take her back to her cell.
We will announce the verdict in a few days."

As they lead me out of the courtroom I see a crowd waiting.
I had no idea my trial would be important.

And there is my mother,
who is risking her life to see me.
She's hiding the yellow star
by holding her purse against her chest.
I throw my arms around her, crying,
but the guard drags me away.
He says we'll be allowed to talk
after sentence has been passed.

"But the sentence has been postponed," I protest.

"Then she can visit you in prison," he says.

Mother follows us down the stairs
and when the guard goes to get the prison car
to take me back to Conti Street prison,
we embrace, tearful and wordless.

26

Driving back to prison in the car,
I stare out of the window hungrily,
wanting to see ordinary people doing ordinary things.

It hurts me to watch the real world outside my window,
but I cling to everything I see
as though it could prolong my life.

27

Why doesn't my mother come to see me?

The prison is almost empty.

My only visitor is a lizard on the wall.
I spend hours waiting for him to come
and keep me company.

A transparent twig
stands on the wall
sleepy as a century

he and the wall
are brothers:
colorless
patient

a flick of membrane

a motion of mind

=29=

Because I'll be leaving soon,
I feel my senses closing down.

I know the sun is shining, the sky is blue,
the stones are shimmering in the noon glare,
but I'm shut behind a black door.

=30=

A messenger from the Hungarian court is here:

"I have come to tell you a verdict has been reached."

"Don't I have to be taken back to court?
Shouldn't the verdict be made in public?"

"There's no time."

"No, there's no time. The verdict has been reached
for the Arrow-Cross too. Your punishment will come
when the Russians take over the city."

"Don't be insolent. I'll read the verdict:
The military tribunal has found Hanna Senesh
guilty of treason
and has demanded the supreme penalty."

"Does that mean I'm sentenced to die?"

"You have one hour. You can write a farewell message
if you wish."

"I want to see my mother."

"There isn't time."

"At least let me see my mother."

"We must evacuate the prison. No one
must be left behind."

31

Mother dearest

I can only say this to you: a million thanks.
And forgive me if possible. You alone will understand
why there is no longer any need for words.

                With endless love—your daughter

Truly, there is no need for words, and there are none.

32

I see my mother marching in the cold November rain
with a long bedraggled line of friends, neighbors, strangers,
all carrying their pitiful bundles of blankets, keepsakes,
things they've snatched up in the last moments
before beginning the forced march to Auschwitz.

I know she has slept on the cold ground under the sky
for several days. She is ill.

I see her slip away from the crowd, tear off her yellow star,
step into a shop beside the road.

The shopkeeper, a kind woman, hides her.

Now she is riding back to Budapest,
concealed in a wagon of hay and vegetables.

And now—she is lying in a hospital bed in a convent,
protected by the nuns, who know who she is.

She scarcely wants to live.

Will she die?

A man is coming through the doorway.
It is Joel, my Joel, escaped from the death train,
dressed in rags, but shining.
He holds her visa in his hand.
He takes her tenderly away, across the Danube.

I see water—she is on a ship, coming into port.
It is Haifa, golden Haifa sparkling in the sunlight.

George is waiting for her.

She is home at last.

33

Janos runs in, wringing his hands.

"Everyone is running away. One truck after another is pulling out."

We hear a shot.

"Are they shooting the prisoners?"

"Yes, miss," he says.

34

I can see my body shaking, but inside I feel still.

They lead me to a wooden post
under the open sky.
The guard starts to tie me to it.
I say, "No, I'll stand by myself."

He offers me a blindfold.
I push him away.
I'll look at the world as long as I can.

The November air is cold.
If only my body would stop shaking.

I hear a shot, echoing, far away.

Is it meant for me?

I feel myself grow tall tall tall as the sky

=35=

I'm standing in the ancient ruins at Caesarea
among the shattered Roman columns
lying in seawater
and I see
the broken statue of a woman
missing entirely above the waist:

but I can tell
from the white hand
lifting the folds of her garment,
from her hard thigh
beneath the fluted skirt,
from the sure grace of her bent knee
and the foot she is leaning on
in its imaginary sandal
the foot
taking her weight

I can tell
she is there

inside the broken body
she is complete

Ruth Whitman is a widely published poet, author, and translator. Her works of poetry include Permanent Address *(1980),* Tamsen Donner: A Woman's Journey *(1977),* The Passion of Lizzie Borden *(1973),* The Marriage Wig *(1968), and* Blood & Milk Poems *(1963). She has also written a collection of essays entitled* Becoming a Poet: Source, Process and Practice *(1982) and edited* Poemmaking: Poets in Classrooms. *Her translations include* The Selected Poems of Jacob Glatstein *(1972) and* An Anthology of Modern Yiddish Poetry *(1966). Whitman is lecturer in poetry for Radcliffe Seminars of Radcliffe College. She received her B.A. degree from Radcliffe College and her M.A. from Harvard University.*

Historian Livia Rothkirchen, former editor of the Yad Vashem Studies *from 1968 to 1983, is the author of many monographs on the Jews of Slovakia, Hungary, and Bohemia-Moravia and the author of* The Destruction of Slovak Jewry: A Documentary History. *She lives in Jerusalem.*

The manuscript was edited by Anne M. G. Adamus. The book was designed by Joanne Kinney. The typeface for the text and the display is Galliard.

Manufactured in the United States of America.

WITHDRAWN